Turn
on the
Faucet

. . . .

by Lynn Brunell

BLACKBIRCH®
PRESS

THOMSON

GALE

San Diego • Detroit • New York • San Francisco • Cleveland • New Haven, Conn. • Waterville, Maine • London • Munich

For more information, contact
The Gale Group, Inc.
27500 Drake Rd.
Farmington Hills, MI 48331-3535
Or you can visit our Internet site at http://www.gale.com

LIBRARY OF CONGRESS CATALOGING-IN-PUBLICATION DATA

Brunelle, Lynn.
  Turn on the faucet / by Lynn Brunelle.
      v. cm. — (Step Back Science series)
  Includes bibliographical references and index.
  Contents: A twist of fate: turn on the faucet — Weight matters: water's weight helps it flow behind the sink — Pipe up: hot and cold water separate in pipes behind the wall — Invisible enemies: chlorine kills bacteria and viruses — Time for fall: water falls to earth as precipitation.
    ISBN 1-56711-681-7 (hardback : alk. paper)
  1. Water-supply — Juvenile literature. [1. Water supply.] I. Title. II. Series.
  TD348.B78 2003
  363.6′1—dc1   2002011729

Printed in United States
10 9 8 7 6 5 4 3 2 1

Contents # Turn on the Faucet

How to Use This Book

Each Step Back Science book traces the path of a science-based act backwards, from its result to its beginning.

Each double-page spread like the ones below explains one step in the process.

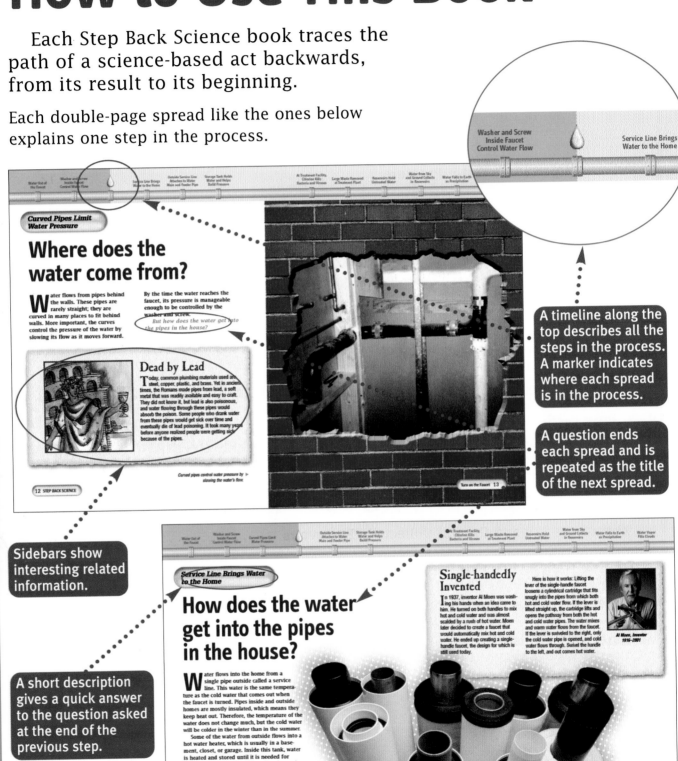

A timeline along the top describes all the steps in the process. A marker indicates where each spread is in the process.

A question ends each spread and is repeated as the title of the next spread.

Sidebars show interesting related information.

A short description gives a quick answer to the question asked at the end of the previous step.

Side Step spreads, like the one below, offer separate but related information.

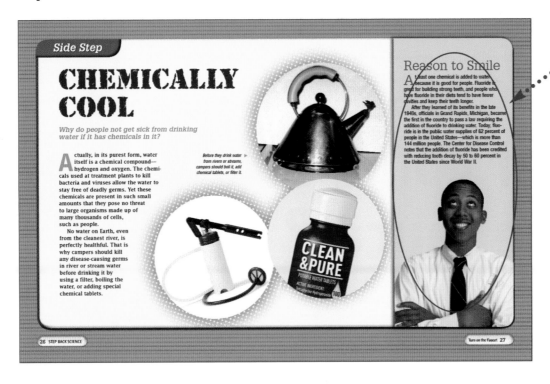

Every Side Step spread contains a sidebar.

The Big Picture, on pages 40–41, shows you the entire process at a glance.

Washer and Screw
Inside Faucet
Control Water Flow

Curved Pipes Limit
Water Pressure

Service Line Brings
Water to the Home

Outside Service Line
Attaches to Water
Main and Feeder Pipe

Storage Tank Holds
Water and Helps
Build Pressure

Water Out of the Faucet

How does water come out of the faucet?

Thirsty? Just give the faucet a twist and voilà! Out comes water.

The simple action of turning on the faucet puts into motion a complex and far-reaching sequence of events. While all you see is the faucet and its handles, behind the scenes there is a world of pipes, tanks, wells, treatment plants, reservoirs, and even clouds that make it possible for water to flow when a handle is turned.

So why does turning the handle make water come out?

Drain

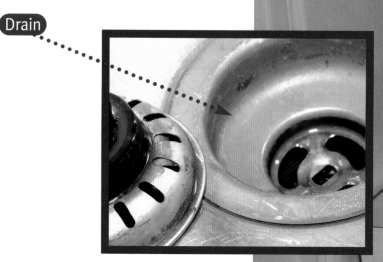

At Treatment Facility, Chlorine Kills Bacteria and Viruses

Large Waste Removed at Treatment Plant

Reservoirs Hold Untreated Water

Water from Sky and Ground Collects in Reservoirs

Water Falls to Earth as Precipitation

Water Vapor Fills Clouds

Hot and Cold Handles

Spout

Water Out of
the Faucet

Curved Pipes Limit
Water Pressure

Service Line Brings
Water to the Home

Outside Service Line
Attaches to Water
Main and Feeder Pipe

Storage Tank Holds
Water and Helps
Build Pressure

Washer and Screw Inside Faucet Control Water Flow

Why does turning the handle make water come out?

Turning the handle twists a screw inside the faucet, which activates the tiny "on/off" system of the faucet. When the faucet is off, the screw holds a washer—a flat disk made of metal, plastic, rubber, or leather—against a hole in the pipe inside a faucet. When the handle is turned, the screw is turned. This lifts the washer and lets water flow through the hole and out the faucet spout.

A reverse turn of the handle stops the water. This twisting motion pushes the screw against the washer, which closes up the hole in the pipe and prevents water from flowing through.

But where does the water come from?

Spout

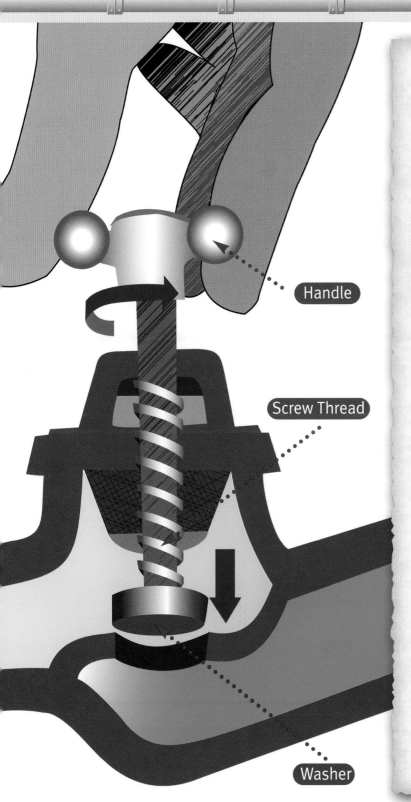

Handle

Screw Thread

Washer

▲ *The remains of a Roman-style aqueduct in Turkey.*

Public Service

The Romans were among the first to build water pipelines. According to archeologists who studied the ancient city of Pompeii, Mount Vesuvius erupted and covered the city in hot ash in A.D. 79. It killed the people but preserved the city. The archeologists found that the ancient Romans created aqueducts—channels or passageways designed to transport water from a remote source, usually by gravity—that moved water to lead pipes that flowed into people's homes in Pompeii.

Faucets were not found in the average home. Yet faucets made of silver, marble, and gold were found in Pompeii's luxurious public baths.

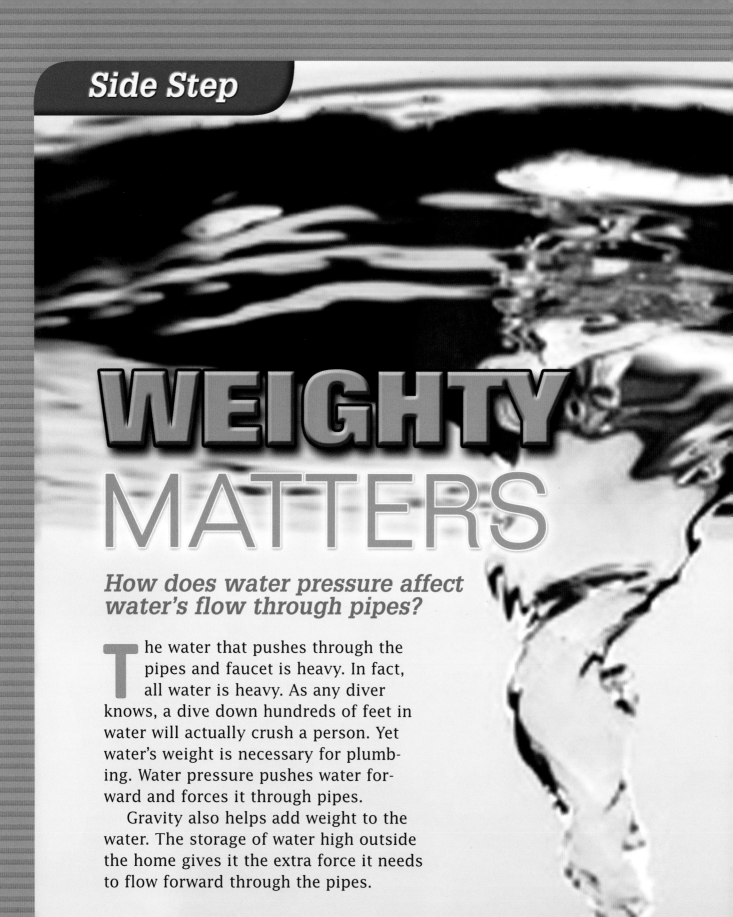

WEIGHTY MATTERS

How does water pressure affect water's flow through pipes?

The water that pushes through the pipes and faucet is heavy. In fact, all water is heavy. As any diver knows, a dive down hundreds of feet in water will actually crush a person. Yet water's weight is necessary for plumbing. Water pressure pushes water forward and forces it through pipes.

Gravity also helps add weight to the water. The storage of water high outside the home gives it the extra force it needs to flow forward through the pipes.

▲ *U-turn pipes with traps below are designed for safety and convenience.*

Down the Drain

Pipes not only bring water to the sink, but also carry it away. In some sink models, a pipe leads from the drain, comes straight down, does a U-turn back up, and then makes another turn before it disappears behind the wall. The U-turn curve is important for at least two reasons. The curve itself prevents smelly gases, such as methane and sulfur from rotten food, from coming up through the pipes. The very bottom of it has a safety device called the trap because it traps solid materials like jewelry or contact lenses that might accidentally fall down the drain and block the flow of water. Plumbers and handy homeowners can unscrew part of the trap to remove items and reopen water flow.

The kitchen drain, bathroom drains, and toilets all have pipes leading out of the house. These pipes are on a downward slope, so that gravity pushes the water out of the house. Once the pipes lead out of the house, they join a larger pipe called the sewer main. All the homes on a street connect with the main, and the dirty water is pushed along to the treatment plants where it is cleaned up and put back into the system.

Curved Pipes Limit Water Pressure

Where does the water come from?

Water flows from pipes behind the walls. These pipes are rarely straight; they are curved in many places to fit behind walls. More important, the curves control the pressure of the water by slowing its flow as it moves forward.

By the time the water reaches the faucet, its pressure is manageable enough to be controlled by the washer and screw.

But how does the water get into the pipes in the house?

Dead by Lead

Today, common plumbing materials used are steel, copper, plastic, and brass. Yet in ancient times, the Romans made pipes from lead, a soft metal that was readily available and easy to craft. They did not know it, but lead is also poisonous, and water flowing through these pipes would absorb the poison. Some people who drank water from these pipes would get sick over time and eventually die of lead poisoning. It took many years before anyone realized people were getting sick because of the pipes.

Curved pipes control water pressure by ▶
slowing the water's flow.

At Treatment Facility,
Chlorine Kills
Bacteria and Viruses

Large Waste Removed
at Treatment Plant

Reservoirs Hold
Untreated Water

Water from Sky
and Ground Collects
in Reservoirs

Water Falls to Earth
as Precipitation

Water Vapor
Fills Clouds

Service Line Brings Water to the Home

How does the water get into the pipes in the house?

Water flows into the home from a single pipe outside called a service line. This water is the same temperature as the cold water that comes out when the faucet is turned. Pipes inside and outside homes are mostly insulated, which means they keep heat out. Therefore, the temperature of the water does not change much, but the cold water will be colder in the winter than in the summer.

Some of the water from outside flows into a hot water heater, which is usually in a basement, closet, or garage. Inside this tank, water is heated and stored until it is needed for baths, showers, hand-washings, laundry, and dishwashers. If a hot water faucet handle is turned, hot water will make its way through a pipe attached to the heater and into the pipe attached to the faucet. When both the hot and cold water handles are turned at the same time, the water mixes to create warm water.

So how does the water get inside the service line?

Single-handedly Invented

In 1937, inventor Al Moen was washing his hands when an idea came to him. He turned on both handles to mix hot and cold water and was almost scalded by a rush of hot water. Moen later decided to create a faucet that would automatically mix hot and cold water. He ended up creating a single-handle faucet, the design for which is still used today.

Here is how it works: Lifting the lever of the single-handle faucet loosens a cylindrical cartridge that fits snugly into the pipes from which both hot and cold water flow. If the lever is lifted straight up, the cartridge lifts and opens the pathway from both the hot and cold water pipes. The water mixes and warm water flows from the faucet. If the lever is swiveled to the right, only the cold water pipe is opened, and cold water flows through. Swivel the handle to the left, and out comes hot water.

Al Moen, Inventor 1916–2001

◀ *Pipes in different sizes are surrounded by insulation to maintain water temperature.*

HOT STUFF

How is water heated in the home?

Most homes have a water heater. Some homes have a tankless heater that has powerful burners to heat water as it flows through copper coils in the pipes, but most homes have a water heater tank. In these systems, a large, cylindrical tank holds water and uses electricity or gas to heat it.

Cold water flows into the tank and sinks to the bottom. As the water is heated, hot water rises to the top. The thermostat keeps the water heated at a specific temperature while the pipe near the top of the tank carries water throughout the home. Cold water is always flowing into the tank as water is being used and released from the tank. Still, if someone takes a long, hot shower or leaves the hot water running, it is possible to remove the hot water so fast that the cold water does not have enough time to heat up. The home will then be left with cold water until more water can be heated.

Parts of a Heater

Drain valve: valve that can be opened to drain water from the tank, if repairs are needed

Heater: part that heats the water

Inner tank: tank where water is heated and held before it flows into a faucet

Insulation dip tube: tube that brings cold water into the tank

Pipe: passageway for hot water to leave the tank and flow to a faucet

Pressure relief valve: safety valve that releases pressure so the tank will not explode

Sacrificial anode rod: rod that corrodes inside the tank, which prevents the interior walls of the tank from rusting

Thermostat: gauge that allows adjustments to water temperature

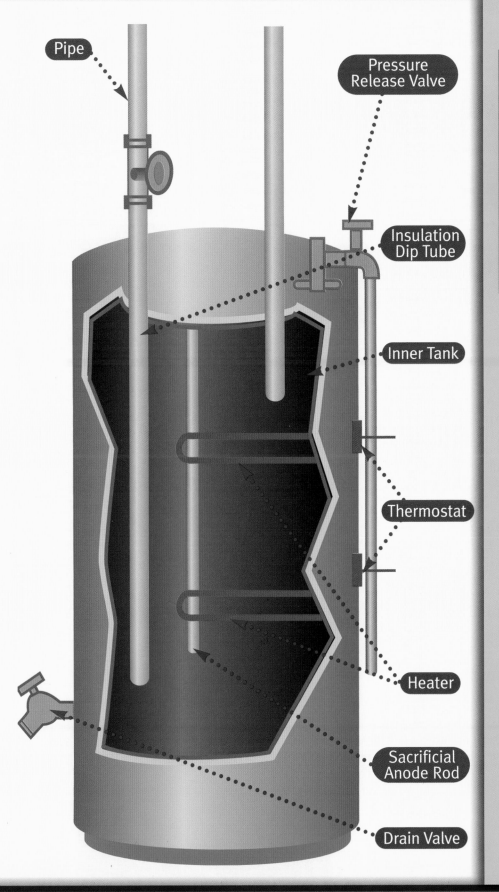

Pipe

Pressure
Release Valve

Insulation
Dip Tube

Inner Tank

Thermostat

Heater

Sacrificial
Anode Rod

Drain Valve

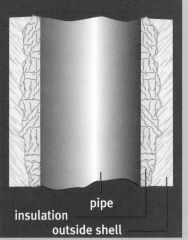

pipe
insulation
outside shell

Crack-up

In parts of the country that get cold in the winter, the pipes behind the wall or under the sink might be covered in insulated heat tape and further protected by a layer of insulation. All this insulation is used because frozen pipes are a major wintertime worry. When water gets below 32° F (0° C), it freezes, turns solid, and expands, which may create a blockage in a pipe that will prevent water from flowing. If this happens, pressure builds up behind the blockage and over time the pipes will crack or simply break. Water could then leak through the pipes and cause flooding.

Water Out of
the Faucet

Washer and Screw
Inside Faucet
Control Water Flow

Curved Pipes Limit
Water Pressure

Service Line Brings
Water to the Home

Storage Tank Holds
Water and Helps
Build Pressure

**Outside Service Line Attaches
to Water Main and Feeder Pipe**

How does water get inside the service line?

Water flows to the service line from a water main, a larger pipe that branches out and forms a network underground in a community. Water flowing from the water main comes from an extra-large pipe made of concrete, plastic, or metal. The large pipe is generally called a feeder pipe because it feeds water to the community.

The path that water takes to get to homes is long and winding, but the water is under constant pressure to flow forward. To imagine how much pressure is needed, picture an open fire hydrant. Fire hydrants are hooked up directly to water mains, and when they are open, the full force of the water pressure pushes the water fast and far.

But where does the water from the feeder pipe come from?

At Treatment Facility,
Chlorine Kills
Bacteria and Viruses | Large Waste Removed
at Treatment Plant | Reservoirs Hold
Untreated Water | Water from Sky
and Ground Collects
in Reservoirs | Water Falls to Earth
as Precipitation | Water Vapor
Fills Clouds

Measure Maker

There is a price to pay for clean drinking water. Communities that clean and treat water measure how much water people use and charge accordingly. Before the water gets to the faucet, it flows past a water meter that measures how much water flows into a home. As soon as a faucet is turned or a toilet flushed, water flows and the meter measures it. If the pipes happen to have a leak, that gets measured as well.

As water passes through the meter's monitor, it turns the blades on a tiny wheel inside, which turns a shaft, which turns tiny gears, which rotate the drums of a counter with numbers on them. These numbers reflect the total volume of water that has flowed through the pipes, and customers who use the water supply pay based on these numbers.

Storage Tank Holds Water and Helps Build Pressure

Where does the water from the feeder pipe come from?

This large pipe connects to a single source: usually a storage tank. Much of the pressure the water is under builds up here.

Storage tanks are huge water containers that stand on stilts or high atop buildings. Storing water in a high place allows gravity to create enough constant pressure to make water flow through the pipes of a community. The weight of all the water in the tank, due to gravity's downward force, puts a lot of weight on the water at the bottom. By the time water is released from the bottom of the tanks through an opening that connects to the large pipe, it is ready to flow with force.

These tanks are so big—they hold up to 50 times the amount of water in a backyard swimming pool—because each one stores enough water to serve a community for about a day. A high-pressure pump continually lifts water from a local body of water through a pipe that leads into the tower, so the supply in the storage tank does not run out.

In big cities like New York, many apartment

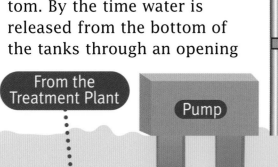

Water

From the Treatment Plant

Pump

To Primary Feeders and Customers

buildings are so high that they have their own storage tanks on the rooftop in order to provide enough water pressure for residents to have constant running water. In the case of these unique systems, water flows from the service line pipe to the tank through a system of pumps, and then it is released to residents through pipes within the building.

Wherever it is stored, the water in a storage tank is clean enough for homeowners.

So how is the water cleaned?

▼ *Community water tanks loom over the landscape like huge sculptures.*

Experiment: Weigh to Go

Materials: Foam cup, pen

Poke four small holes (all the same size and equally distanced) along the side of a foam cup. Make sure one hole is near the bottom and one is near the top, and the holes are large enough to allow water to flow out of them.

Fill the cup with water and hold it over a sink so you can see how water will flow out of the holes. Which hole has the farthest flowing stream?

The bottom hole shoots water the farthest because the weight of water is greatest at the bottom of the cup. Gravity pulls all the water down and the water at the bottom is under the most pressure. More weight and more pressure produce a greater flow.

OCONOMOWOC
A PUBLIC POWER COMMUNITY

GAFFNEY GAFFNEY

WISHING FOR A WELL

What is a well and why are wells needed?

Wells are holes dug into the ground deep enough to reach water under the earth called groundwater. After it seeps through soil and rocks, water stores in underground spaces called aquifers. People in deserts, plains, or other rural parts of the country often must use well water because they do not have city or town water supply systems. The fact is 48 million people in the United States receive their drinking water from private wells, and some public water systems pump groundwater to increase their supply.

A well hole can be dug out by hand, drilled by machine, or created by driving a pipe into the ground until it hits water. Pumps are then installed inside the hole to pull the water up.

Well owners need to test their water and keep it clean. Since the water is below ground, it is often less polluted than surface water, but it is not necessarily pure. Underground, the water mixes with minerals and chemicals, such as fertilizers used in farming. For this reason, well water has to be cleaned and disinfected before it is drinkable.

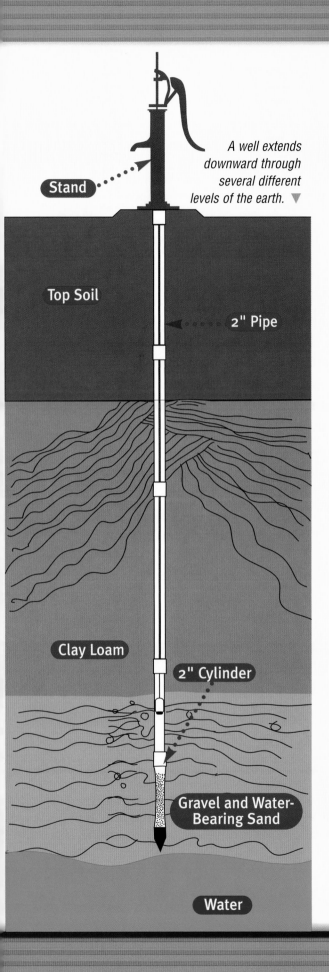

A well extends downward through several different levels of the earth. ▼

Stand

Top Soil

2" Pipe

Clay Loam

2" Cylinder

Gravel and Water-Bearing Sand

Water

All Bottled Up

Many people choose bottled water as a healthy alternative to water from the faucet. The truth is that it may not actually be healthier or purer. Water from any source may contain dust particles, minerals from the earth, or living things that go unseen by the human eye.

While bottled water must pass federal health guidelines, not all bottled water is the same. Fortunately for consumers, the labels on the bottles tell a lot about what is inside. Here is a list of what is what:

IF THE LABEL SAYS	WHAT'S INSIDE THE BOTTLE
Drinking water	Water from an approved source, which means it meets federal and state standards. It has been filtered and probably disinfected.
Mineral water	Water collected and bottled right where water comes up from a protected underground source. It has at least 250 milligrams of natural minerals and trace elements per liter. Additional minerals cannot be added.
Well water	Water pumped from a well that taps into groundwater.
Artesian water	Water collected naturally from a well that taps into groundwater. (The pressure of the underground water pushes it up into the well, so no pump is needed.)
Spring water	Water tapped and collected directly from an underground source.
Purified water	Water that was treated, filtered, disinfected, and purified.
Distilled water	Water that has been boiled into steam and then condensed.
Sparkling water	Water that contains the same amount of carbon dioxide bubbles that it had at the point of emergence from its source.

At Treatment Facility, Chlorine Kills Bacteria and Viruses

How is the water cleaned?

Before water is ready to be pumped into towers and used by homeowners, it has to be treated and cleaned at a water treatment facility, which is linked to the storage tank by pipes. Every day, treatment plants in the United States purify over 35 billion gallons of water. Even the clearest, freshest-looking water collected directly from a mountain river can be full of bacteria and viruses that are too small for the eye to see. For the most part, they do not cause any harm. When they build up inside living organisms, however, they can make people and animals sick.

There are several steps that help get rid of microscopic organisms. One of the best ways to kill them is by using chlorine, the same chemical used to keep swimming pool water clean. Machines add small amounts of chlorine to water treatment tanks to kill bacteria and viruses that cause waterborne diseases. Some water treatment plants also use small amounts of iodine or even ultraviolet light to kill germs.

So how are bigger things cleaned out of the water?

▲ At a modern water treatment plant like the one at left, special equipment called reverse osmosis units (above) filter impurities out of water.

Here's to Health!

In the late 1990s, *Life* magazine cited what it felt was "probably the most significant public health advance of the millennium." The advance was the filtration of drinking water and the use of chlorine to kill water-borne diseases.

Chlorine was first added to drinking water in 1908 mainly to combat the large number of deaths associated with typhoid fever. The disease spread through the water supply and caused many water drinkers to have such high fevers that eventually their internal organs began to fail. At the time, an average of 25 out of every 100,000 people in the United States died from typhoid annually. Within 50 years of the addition of chlorine, however, typhoid fever had almost been eliminated in the United States.

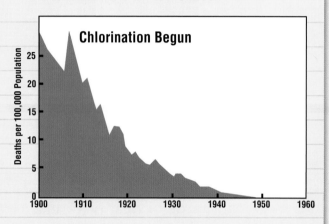

▲ The main control panel monitors and regulates the amount of chemicals put into the water.

▲ Treated water is tested in a lab to make sure it is free from harmful bacteria.

▲ Powerful pumps deliver drinkable water to a distribution system, which in turn carries it to homes and businesses.

CHEMICALLY COOL

Why do people not get sick from drinking water if it has chemicals in it?

Actually, in its purest form, water itself is a chemical compound—hydrogen and oxygen. The chemicals used at treatment plants to kill bacteria and viruses allow the water to stay free of deadly germs. Yet these chemicals are present in such small amounts that they pose no threat to large organisms made up of many thousands of cells, such as people.

No water on Earth, even from the cleanest river, is perfectly healthful. That is why campers should kill any disease-causing germs in river or stream water before drinking it by using a filter, boiling the water, or adding special chemical tablets.

Before they drink water from rivers or streams, campers should boil it, add chemical tablets, or filter it. ▶

Reason to Smile

A t least one chemical is added to water because it is good for people. Fluoride is great for building strong teeth, and people who have fluoride in their diets tend to have fewer cavities and keep their teeth longer.

After they learned of its benefits in the late 1940s, officials in Grand Rapids, Michigan, became the first in the country to pass a law requiring the addition of fluoride to drinking water. Today, fluoride is in the public water supplies of 62 percent of people in the United States—which is more than 144 million people. The Center for Disease Control notes that the addition of fluoride has been credited with reducing tooth decay by 50 to 60 percent in the United States since World War II.

Large Waste Removed at Treatment Plant

How are big things cleaned out of the water?

When water is collected, it is full of dirt particles, bits of leaves, and litter, and these are the first things to be removed at the treatment plant. There are several steps to removing the unnecessary dirt and waste.

1 The water is pushed into a huge basin where it is mixed with chemicals like alum. Alum is a molecule that collects and combines dirt particles. The dirt and alum come together in a process called coagulation to form bigger, heavier globs of dirt, mud, and alum called floc.

2 The next step of the process is called sedimentation. The water and floc mixture is passed along into the settling basin, where the water sits quietly so the heavy floc globs can sink to the bottom of the tank. The cleaner water on top is sent to the next stage.

3 Filtration comes next. In this step, water is passed through gravel, sand, and carbon charcoal filters. These filters trap tiny dirt grains, dust particles, algae, and even some bacteria.

So where is water held before it is cleaned?

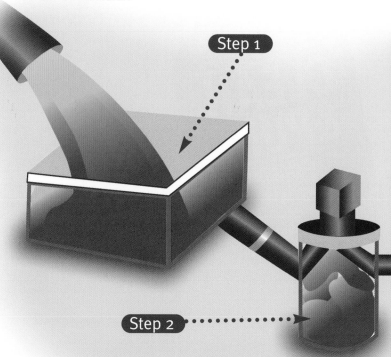

Step 1

Step 2

Step 1 Dirt coagulates into big globs

Step 2 Globs sink in sedimentation

Step 3 Water passes through gravel filter

Step 4 Water passes through sand filter

Step 5 Water passes through carbon charcoal filter

Step 6 Water is purified and pumped back into water supply

Treat It Right

Depending on where people live, they might still find that their drinking water tastes or smells odd even thought it has been treated and purified at the water treatment center. In some parts of the country, the amounts of calcium, zinc, chlorine, and even sediment in water may add a slight flavor or make it smell. This is why some homeowners have a drinking water filtration system built onto their faucet or inside a container. These systems use small particles of charcoal carbon to trap molecules, including chlorine.

A pitcher with a built-in filter provides easy purification.

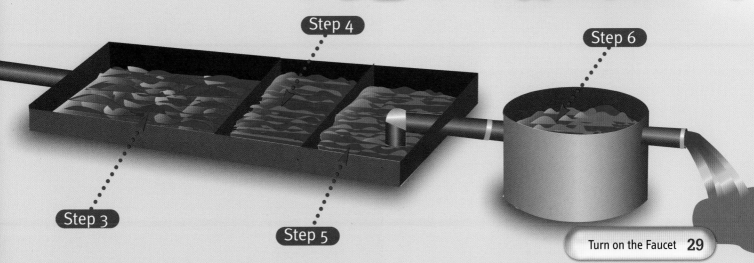

Step 4

Step 6

Step 3

Step 5

Water Out of
the Faucet

Washer and Screw
Inside Faucet
Control Water Flow

Curved Pipes Limit
Water Pressure

Service Line Brings
Water to the Home

How Does Water
Get Inside the
Service Line?

Storage Tank Holds
Water and Helps
Build Pressure

Reservoirs Hold Untreated Water

Where is water held before it is cleaned?

Water collects in reservoirs that are connected by pipes and pumps to the treatment facility. These bodies of water may be artificially made (a cement holding pool) or naturally created (a lake).

Fences protect reservoirs and the land around them. Water inspectors may also monitor reservoirs so people and animals cannot get close enough to contaminate or harm the water with waste, garbage, or harmful chemicals. Usually, plants and trees surround a reservoir to protect the water from soaking up dirt and dust blown by the wind.

So how does the water collect in reservoirs?

Reservoirs are often ▶ off-limits to swimmers and boaters to ensure that the water remains clean.

▲ Dust-covered homes and farms were abandoned by the thousands in the so-called "Dust Bowl."

No Doubt a Drought

Back in the 1930s, people in North America's Southern Great Plains learned what life would be like without water. It did not rain for many months and the air was hot and dry day after day. This caused a severe drought that eventually killed the plants. Because the soil had no plant roots or moisture to anchor it, and animals had severely overgrazed the land, winds that swept the plains blew the dirt for miles and miles, which covered towns, farms, and cities with dust. People called this part of the country the Dust Bowl. By 1939, the drought's effects were largely under control as rain began to fall more regularly and newly planted trees helped control the wind from blowing the dirt.

Water from Sky and Ground Collects in Reservoirs

How does the water collect in reservoirs?

There are several paths that water can take before it reaches one of these bodies of water. Water travels over land, drops from the sky, and flows underground to collect in reservoirs.

As rain or other precipitation falls from the clouds, it hits the ground and seeps into the earth. From there, it can move on land several ways. Water in trees and plants may go back into the atmosphere in a process called transpiration. Water may also gather in puddles and run along the surface of the earth before joining streams and rivers that connect to the reservoir by tunnels or canals. These areas of land where the surface water from rainfall drains into a lake, river, or stream are called watersheds. Groundwater in streams underground may flow toward the reservoir. Water that falls in cities flows down gutters and streets and eventually into drainage or sewer systems. These drains take the water to the sea or to the reservoir.

So how does water get to the earth?

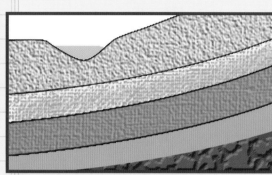

▲ *Layers of soil act as natural filters.*

A Dirty Job

Soil is more than just dirt. It is made up of layers of eroded rocks, minerals, and the remains of once-living things. Many different kinds of soil (sand, peat, chalk, and clay) exist in different places on the earth. Near the surface, the particles are smaller, while deeper down, the rocks and minerals tend to get bigger and bigger. When water seeps through the soil, it passes through these layers. Each layer acts as a separate filter to keep particles and contaminants behind as cleaner water makes its way through pockets in the rock into the groundwater beneath the deepest layers.

NOT SO READY TO SERVE

How much water is available for drinking?

By some estimates, there are over 325 million trillion gallons (325,000,000,000,000,000,000 gallons) on Earth. However, not all of it can be used as drinking water.

Oceans not only cover about 70 percent of the earth's surface, but also make up 98 percent of the earth's water. This water, however, is not drinkable because of all the salt. That means about 2 percent of the entire planet's water is fresh, and some of that is frozen solid at the North and South Poles.

Less than a half percent of all water on Earth makes up drinking water. It is found in underground aquifers, lakes, and rivers. That may not seem like a lot, but it is still a few thousand trillion gallons.

Drinking Water
0.5%

Fresh Water
1.5%

Ocean Water
98%

▲ *Machinery at a desalination plant makes salt water fresh.*

Dry Idea

People cannot drink salt water because salt dries out the body. It soaks up the water with which it comes in contact and causes dehydration. About two-thirds of the human body is water, and humans need to keep that amount constant to make sure their blood flows, skin breathes, and organs work properly. The body inherently knows salt water is bad for it. If people drink too much salt water, they will throw up soon after when their body rejects it.

To make salt water fresh, a person could boil it, collect the steam, and cool it until it becomes fresh water. Water treatment plants where this is done are called desalination plants, and they produce both water and salt for later consumer use.

Water Falls to Earth as Precipitation

How does water get to the earth?

The water that collects in streams, puddles, oceans, reservoirs, plants, and on land comes from precipitation—rain, snow, sleet, and hail. Precipitation is just one part of the water cycle, a natural process in which all of the water on Earth is always changing forms as it moves from the earth to the atmosphere.

Precipitation comes from clouds. These puffy sky-dwellers are actually frozen piles of water vapor, or gas.

So how does water vapor form and collect in a cloud?

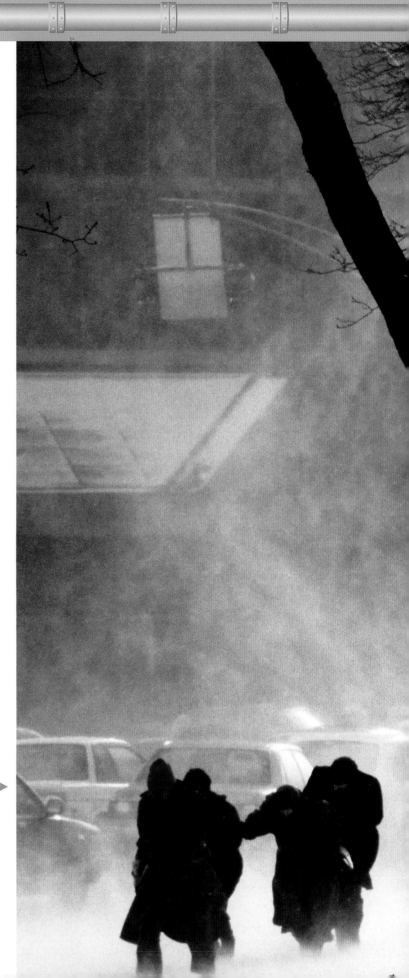

Stormy weather is a ▶ natural part of water's cycle through different forms.

City Slickers

How is rainfall captured in a city—made mostly of concrete, asphalt, and glass? It cannot seep into the ground, but much of it flows into storm drains—holes under a curb in the street or sidewalk that allow the water to flow. In the drain, twigs, trash, and other items are filtered out as the water flows through large metal strainers. From there, it is taken along with other wastewater to a treatment facility to be cleaned, disinfected, and routed back into the system.

Water Vapor Fills Clouds

How does water vapor form and collect in a cloud?

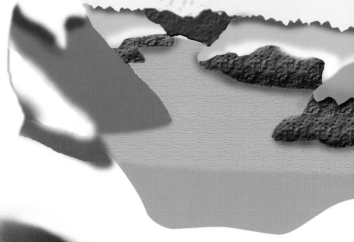

Condensation

Precipitation

As the sun heats up water on Earth, water vapor is formed. This vapor looks and acts a lot like the steam that collects on a bathroom mirror after a hot shower. The tiny gaseous molecules of water rise into the atmosphere to reach cooler temperatures in a process called evaporation.

The vapor molecules in the sky gather around floating dust or other particles, such as those from pollutants or plant materials, to form droplets. The gathered water droplets form a cloud. Because the temperature in the atmosphere is so cold, the droplets may even turn to ice inside the cloud. The process in which water changes from a gas to a liquid or a solid is called condensation.

When clouds can no longer hold growing amounts of water and ice that are collecting in them, bits of liquid or solid water—raindrops or snowflakes—fall to the earth. As they fall, they warm up and sometimes turn back into water drops or a mixture of rain and snow called sleet.

At Treatment Facility, Chlorine Kills Bacteria and Viruses | Large Waste Removed at Treatment Plant | Reservoirs Hold Untreated Water | Water from Sky and Ground Collects in Reservoirs | Water Falls to Earth as Precipitation

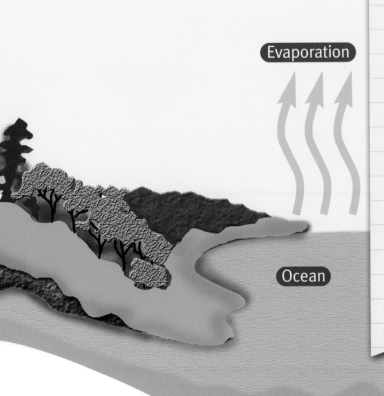

Evaporation

Ocean

The Rainmakers

Some places on Earth get a lot more rain than others. There are three major players in the rain game: the sun, the equator, and the oceans. Oddly enough, Earth could not have its wettest places without its driest places.

Dry places are called deserts. Most deserts are located between 5 and 30 degrees north and south of the equator, the invisible line around the middle of the earth. Air near the equator is warmest because the Sun strikes it most directly. The warm air rises and moves toward the poles. Earth's rotation creates smaller wind currents around the globe. These convection currents produce westerly wind flows in some areas and easterly wind flows in others. Deserts lie between the easterly and westerly wind currents because these areas get little wind and thus little moisture.

The wettest places on Earth are tropical zones, which include rain forests. These areas get a lot of wind so moisture readily flows up to the atmosphere and more precipitation is possible.

▲ *Desert-dwelling animals like camels can store water in their bodies for many days.*

The Big Picture

Follow the path of water from the faucet to the sky.

⑫ Water Out of the Faucet

A faucet handle is turned.
(pages 6–7)

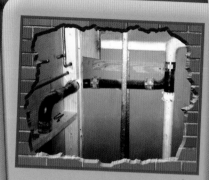

⑩ Curved Pipes Limit Water Pressure

Twisted pipes behind the wall where the sink is located control the flowing water's pressure.
(pages 12–13)

⑧ Outside Service Line Attaches to Water Main and Feeder Pipe

Before it reaches homes, water is pushed through a water main and a large feeder pipe.
(pages 18–19)

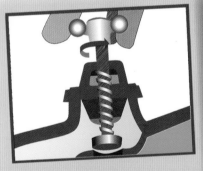

⑪ Washer and Screw Inside Faucet Control Water Flow

Water flows through the faucet because the twist of the handle releases a screw and washer that would otherwise rest against a hole inside the pipe in the faucet.
(pages 8–9)

⑨ Service Line Brings Water to the Home

Water enters the home through a service line pipe. It is cold, but in the home, some water flows into a separate tank where it is heated and stored for use when the hot water handle of the faucet is turned.
(pages 14–15)

⑦ Storage Tank Holds Water and Helps Build Pressure

Storage tanks—located in high places so gravity can create the pressure that helps the flow of water—hold water before it flows to local pipes.
(pages 20–21)

6 At Treatment Facility, Chlorine Kills Bacteria and Viruses

Water is cleaned at a treatment facility, where chemicals such as chlorine are added to kill disease-causing germs.

(pages 24–25)

4 Reservoirs Hold Untreated Water

Before it can be cleaned, water is stored in a reservoir, which is located next to the treatment facility.

(pages 30–31)

2 Water Falls to Earth as Precipitation

All water comes to the earth the same way. As clouds fill with water, they become heavy, break open, and release precipitation.

(pages 36–37)

5 Large Waste Removed at Treatment Plant

At the treatment facility, larger dirt and waste are cleaned out first.

(pages 28–29)

3 Water from Sky and Ground Collects in Reservoirs

Water collects in a reservoir from nearby bodies of water, groundwater, sewer systems linked by pipes, or precipitation.

(pages 32–33)

1 Water Vapor Fills Clouds

Water vapor from the earth evaporates into the atmosphere, cools off, and condenses, forming clouds.

(pages 38–39)

The Water-ful World of Water

Water World Records

The driest place on Earth is the Atacama Desert in Chile. Oddly enough, icy Antarctica is also a very dry place. Although it is covered by glaciers that hold much of the earth's fresh water, the water is frozen and the climate is so cold that the continent gets little precipitation. Meanwhile, the rainiest place on Earth is in Hawaii on Mount Waialeale, which averages 460 inches (1168 cm.) of rain a year.

Leaky Loser

Approximately 20 percent of the drinking water supply in the United States is lost through leaky faucets and toilets. When a faucet drips water, it is most likely the fault of a broken washer. As washers get old, they often crack. Water will then seep around the cracks and drip into the sink. Those little drips can add up. One leaky faucet could drip up to 10 gallons (38 liters) of water a day.

Bodies of Water

💧 Americans drink more than a billion glasses of water a day.

💧 The human body is almost 75 percent water.

💧 In one hot day, a human body can lose up to four pints (1.9 liters) of sweat, which is mostly water.

💧 Babies need to drink almost seven times as much water per pound as an average adult.

Far Out Plumbing

Fresh water is a big concern on the International Space Station, which floats in space without gravity. No gravity means no movement of water. To create plumbing for the station, designers laid out tubes, pipes, and ducts between the station's outer skin and its inner walls to circulate water and air.

Because the station only has a fixed amount of water and air inside it, both elements must be recycled. In fact, the urine of the crew and laboratory animals is purified and added back to the station's drinking supply.

Astronauts store drinking water in a sealed container, much like a juice bag. The container can be hooked up to a dispenser that allows the astronauts to select how much water they want and then push a button to suck it out.

The Global Pool

At any given time of day, there is enough water vapor in the atmosphere that if it fell to the earth as rain all at once, the entire planet would be covered with about 1 inch (2.54 cm.) of water all the way around.

WATER, WATER EVERYWHERE

Thanks to the water cycle, there is a lot of water on and around the earth every day.

• It is always raining somewhere in the 48 contiguous, or connected, United States. On average, about 4 cubic miles (about 6 cubic kilometers) of precipitation fall in the United States each day. That is enough to fill over 7 million Olympic-size* pools!

• Every day, about 300 cubic miles (about 500 cubic kilometers) of water evaporates into the atmosphere. That is more water than can fill over 500 million Olympic-size swimming pools!

*An Olympic-size swimming pool is filled with 609,000 gallons (2,314,200 liters) of water.

Wonders and Words

Questions and Answers

Q: *Do water towers freeze in the winter?*

A: In places like Montana and North Dakota where temperatures dip far below freezing for many weeks in a row, the water in the water towers does freeze. Engineers must install heating systems in the towers to prevent them from filling with ice. Heat is introduced in the bottom, and since heat rises, warm water rises to the top of the tower. Water at the very top of the tank might freeze, but there is always liquid water in the tank.

Q: *In a bathroom, why does the faucet's water temperature sometimes change when the toilet is flushed?*

A: When you flush a toilet, the tank behind the bowl empties and pushes the waste down pipes into the sewer system. New water then rushes in to refill the toilet tank and the bowl. The flush causes water to rush out of the cold water pipe so quickly that it results in a drop in water pressure and flow for the whole home's hot and cold water supply. Depending on the structure of the plumbing, either hot water or cold water then may dominate in some of the home's plumbing lines until the water pressure equalizes.

Q: *What happens in parts of the country where the drinking water has more minerals than in other parts of the country?*

A: Hard water is water that is high in dissolved minerals, such as calcium and magnesium, which have been picked up as water seeps through the earth. Some communities have more of these minerals than others do because of their location and the work done (or not done) by their treatment plants. Hard water will not hurt living things, but it can make soap less sudsy, hair feel limp, and add a grimy buildup on faucets and sinks. Filters, chemicals, and water softeners can be used to get rid of these problems.

Q: *How long can the same drinking water be used?*

A: All the water on Earth has been around for billions of years. The same water that comes down to the ground as rain and is used by plants and animals, soaked into the ground, or gathered in lakes, rivers, and oceans is forever recycled back into the atmosphere where it can again fall to Earth. The water is the same water that our ancestors used and that the dinosaurs drank.

Glossary

Aqueducts: Channels or passageways designed to transport water from a remote source, usually by gravity.

Aquifer: An underground layer of porous earth or stone that stores water.

Chlorine: Chemical added to water at the treatment facility in order to kill bacteria and viruses.

Coagulation: Soft particles of dirt sticking together to make a more solid mass.

Condensation: Water in a gas form cooling off and coming together to form liquid water.

Evaporation: The process in which water heats up to become water vapor.

Filtration: The process of sifting particles out of a liquid.

Floc: A mass formed in water by suspended particles.

Gravity: Natural force pulling all things toward the center of the earth.

Groundwater: Water that seeps through the earth's surface through cracks and spaces between rocks to form bodies of water underground.

Hot water heater: Tank in which water is heated and stored until a hot water handle is turned.

Insulated: Keeps in heat or cold.

Precipitation: Water, snow, sleet, or hail that forms in a cloud and falls to Earth.

Reservoir: Artificially created or natural lake used for collecting and holding water before it is treated for drinking water.

Sedimentation: The sinking of heavy particles.

Service line: Pipe that runs from the water main pipe to a home.

Storage tank: Large tank in which water is stored after being cleaned.

Surface water: Water on the surface of the earth, such as lakes, ponds, rivers, and oceans.

Transpiration: The process of water vapor passing to the atmosphere through the leaves in plants.

Washer: Flat disk made of metal, plastic, rubber, or leather, that is commonly placed beneath a screw's nut to relieve friction, prevent leakage, or distribute pressure.

Water main: Pipe that runs from a large feeder pipe that is connected to the storage tank to a service line.

Watershed: Area where rain and surface water drain into a specific river, lake, or spring.

Water vapor: Water in the gas state.

Index

Credits:

Produced by: J. A. Ball Associates, Inc.
Jacqueline Ball, Justine Ciovacco
Daniel H. Franck, Ph.D., Science Consultant

Art Direction, Design, and Production:
designlabnyc
Todd Cooper, Sonia Gauba

Writer: Lynn Brunelle

Cover: Brooke Fasani: washing dishes; John Garbarini Photography: pipes; Jim Cook/Cherokee County Chamber of Commerce, Gaffney, SC: peach-shaped water tank; Doug Keller/Water Department, Sandusky, OH: water treatment facility; Corel: mountains.

Interior: Brooke Fasani: p.6 washing dishes, p.29 pouring water; Sonia Gauba: p.8 diagram of faucet, p.16 diagram of water heater, diagram of pipe insulation, p.20 diagram of water tank, p.23 diagram of well, p.28 diagram of waste removal; p.33 diagram of soil layers, p.34 chart graphic, p.39 diagram of evaporation; Photospin: p.6 drain, p.21 water tank, lower left, p.31 reservoir, p.36 snowstorm, p.39 camel, p.42 snow on mountain, p.43 astronaut, tape measure, water, p.44 toilet, bottle; Corel: p.8 aqueduct, p.33 mountain and stream; PhotoDisc, Inc.: p.10 water, p.13 bricks, p.21 clipboard, p.27: boy with toothbrush, p.37 puddle, p.48 water drops; DeRose Enterprises, Inc.: p.11 U-turn pipe; Dino Maniaci: p.12 Roman with goblet; John Garbarini Photography: p.13 pipes; Thermal Pipe Systems: p.14 thermal pipes; Moen Incorporated: p.15 Al Moen; Dan Kochensparger/Upper Arlington Fire Division, Arlington, OH: fire hydrants; Philip Gladstone: p.19 water meter; Jim Cook/Cherokee County Chamber of Commerce, Gaffney, SC: p.21 peach-shaped water tank; Todd Cooper: p.21 water tanks, lower right, p.26 bottle, tea kettle, p.42 faucet; Orange County Water District: p.24 water treatment facility; Doug Keller/Water Department, Sandusky, OH: p.25 water treatment facility; Cascade Designs: p.26 SweetWater Guardian Microfilter; Library of Congress: images of Dust Bowl; Metcalf & Eddy: p.35 desalination plant.

For More Information

U.S. Environmental Protection Agency
www.epa.gov/ow/kids.html
Links, materials, and projects involving water quality and the environment.

U.S. Geological Survey
http://water.usgs.gov
Questions and answers, maps, activities, and links related to water.

The Earth Group. *50 Simple Things Kids Can Do to Save the Earth.* New York: Scholastic, 1990.

Macaulay, David. *The New Way Things Work.* Boston: Houghton Mifflin, 1998.

Shaw McKinney, Barbara. *A Drop Around the World.* Nevada City, Calif.: Dawn Publications, 1998.

Flanagan, Alice K. *Water (Simply Science).* Mankato, Minn.: Compass Point Books, 2000.